By The Sea!
A Kid's Guide to Valletta, Malta

Photography By John D. Weigand
Poetry By Penelope Dyan

Bellissima Publishing, LLC
Jamul, California
www.bellissimapublishing.com

copyright © 2011 by Penny D. Weigand and John D. Weigand

All rights reserved. No part of this book may be reproduced or transmitted in any form or by any means, electronic or mechanical, including photocopying, recording, or by any other means, or by any information or storage retrieval system, without permission from the publisher.

ISBN 978-1-935630-55-5

First Edition

For Travelers everywhere!
Wherever they may be...

By The Sea!
Bellissima Publishing, LLC

Introduction

Malta has been inhabited since it was settled around 5200 BC by ancients from the Italian island of Sicily. Later, the Phoenicians and the Greeks arrived, the Romans and the Arabs, and the French and the English. Malta is a virtual melting pot. The Siege of Malta (also known as the Great Siege of Malta) took place in 1565 when the Ottomans invaded the island, then held by the Knights of Saint John. For the next 275 years, the knights called this island home. They built towns, palaces, churches, and also wall fortifications. Malta is rich in history and is a very fun place to explore and to see. Take time to explore this beautiful island through the words and photography of John D. Weigand and Penelope Dyan and walk the streets of this amazing place as you look through these pages.

This book is meant for children, It is intended to encourage the minds of the young to imagine and to explore; and award winning author and poet Penelope Dyan, who is also an attorney and a former teacher, aims to do just that! Malta is a colorful and amazing place seeped in culture and history that will amaze kids and adults alike.

By The Sea!
Bellissima Publishing, LLC

By The Sea!
A Kid's Guide to Valletta, Malta

Photography By John D. Weigand
Poetry By Penelope Dyan

You can hop on this old time blue bus and see,
Malta as it was meant to be.
This little blue bus will take you all around
into the three cities, and into the town.
And finally when all is said and done,
You will say, "Oh my goodness, Malta was fun!"

There is another mode of transport,
that you can use, of course.
You can take a ride in a covered buggy
pulled by a BEAUTIFUL horse!

Or you can walk through this dark tunnel and take an elevator up to the top floor, and you can see the city gate of Valletta and then see oh so much more!

You can take a car or a taxi,
or you can take a pre-set guided tour on a bus.
Seeing beautiful Malta is really not much fuss.

The island of Malta is beautiful to behold.
And looking down upon NEVER gets old.

There are sailboats and yachts, and ships of many a size,
that you can behold and see with your own two eyes.

There are pizzas and sandwiches,
and sodas. . . and so MANY things sweet.
And you will never, ever go hungry here
because there's so MUCH you can eat!
And you can fill up your little tummy,
with heathy foods that are REALLY yummy!

And don't you think that it is oh so very funny,
that these streets are so very beautiful,
even when it's raining and NOT sunny?
Because even when (in Malta) it is rainy and wet,
this is one beautiful place you will never forget.

You can see a dungeon sitting by the sea,
looking as beautiful and as tranquil as it can be.
As you look through its arches past the shore,
you can see even more for your eyes to explore.

This is the place where
once knights of old did roam.
It's where the Order of Saint John
once made their home.
And all around this island they
built a great wall,
So to invading forces
they would NEVER fall.

If you look very closely,
you will see these boats have eyes,
that will chase away all evil
that comes to them by surprise!

And again you see the majestic wall
(between the sky and the sea) standing so tall.
Protecting knights' and pilgrims' journeys
to the holy land,
with a safe haven of protection
beautiful and grand!

And you will ALL wish, just a LITTLE bit,
Never to leave, when you see Malta at night lit.
And as through the streets and port of Malta
you do carefully wend,
you will know, oh so very sadly,
that you are at last at journey's end.

Parting is such sweet sorrow,
That I shall say good night till it be morrow.
Shakespeare's Romeo And Juliet Act 2, scene 2

www.ingramcontent.com/pod-product-compliance
Lightning Source LLC
LaVergne TN
LVHW070451080526
838202LV00035B/2804